Good Blessed Morning!

Kimberly Dixon Carroll

GOOD BLESSED MORNING!
Copyright © 2019 by Kimberly Dixon Carroll

All rights reserved. No part of this book may be reproduced or transmitted in any form or by any means without written permission from the author.

ISBN: 978-1-7339413-6-5

Scripture Quotations:
New American Standard Bible Copyright © 1960, 1962, 1963, 1968, 1971, 1972, 1973, 1975, 1977, 1995 by The Lockman Foundation, La Habra, Calif. All rights reserved.

Printed in USA by The Vision to Fruition Publishing House (www.vision-fruition.com)

1 Thessalonians 5:11

"Therefore encourage one another and build each other up, just as in fact you are doing."

Deuteronomy 28:12

"The LORD will open to you his good treasury, the heavens, to give the rain to your land in its season and to bless all the work of your hands. And you shall lend to many nations, but you shall not borrow."

TABLE OF CONTENTS

You Were Created to Shine 2
Acknowledgements 3
Foreword 4
I Am Human 5
A Prayer Today 6
My Beautiful Husband 7
Sweet Roll 8
Soulmate 9
Forgiveness 10
Packed Schedules 11
God's Classroom 12
Deceit 14
Joy 16
Filled with Hope 17
Self-Love 18
The Table 19
Ebbs and Flows 20
Eyes of God 21
Greatness 22
Juxtaposition 23
Homelessness 24
Barren Soul 25
Troubled Waters 26
Road of Success 27

Black Family Wealth	28
Recognize Your Value	30
Love Supports	31
The Last First	32
Aligned with God's Purpose	33
Cob Webs	34
Road Traveled	35
My Friend	36
Growing Old	38
Gift of Love	39
Beautiful Queens	40
Miracles of God	41
Our Wedding Moment	42
Light is Bright	43
Welcome to the New	44
We Hope	45
Unique	46
Racism	47
You Are Valuable	48
Blueprint of Peace	49
Confront	50
Our Black Mothers	51
Mother Queens	52
Family	53
Purpose Ordained by God	54
Joy Lives in the Heart	55

Grown	56
All is Well	57
One Race	58
Love Transcends	59
Our Veterans	60
No Doubting	61
God's Happiness	62
Balance of Life	63
Dawn of Hope	64
Pearls of Beauty	65
Empathy	66
Love is Effortless	67
Respect	68
God Sees Our Best	69
Unshakable Joy	70
Black Lives Matter	71
Stay Encouraged	72
Make Your Dreams a Reality	73
What is God Like	74
Rest During Trouble Waters	75
We Are Blessed	76
Remember God's Hand	77
You Belong to God	78
It is Never Too Late	79
God Is Hope	80
Celebrate Our Love Ones	81

Allow Nakedness	82
Think Outside the Box	83
Priority is Key	85
A Coward is not Honorable	86
You Want the Circle of Progress	87
This Old House	88
No More Excuses	89
What is Your Choice Group	90
Great Blessings	91
Sometimes We Are Part of the Problem	92
The Maze	93
Peace of God	94
Transition	95
Cry of the Poor	96
Thank You Daddy	97
Fear Shattered	98
Experiences Build	99
The Oscars	100
Forgiveness	102
I Wish	103
Walk of Success	104
Opposing Forces of Positive and Negative	106
You Are Deeper Than Physical Attraction	108
Our Fine Points and Strengths	109
Good Conquers Evil	110
God Never Counted Me Out	111

That Great Day 112
Look for God in Every Moment 113
Anchored in God 114
Encourage Yourself 115
No Longer a Stranger 116
What Are You Thinking About? 118
Moral Constitution 119
Storms Come Before the Blessings 120
Teach Me 121
The Favor of God 123
Challenges 125
You are Valuable 127
About the Author 130
About the Publisher 132

YOU WERE CREATED TO SHINE

Often you hear the negative thoughts of others when opportunity presents itself and the one with power denies you access.

You may want to walk in shame but instead you walk in strength knowing that you were created by the Creator filled with intellect, greatness and skills!

No one can make you as small as they desire because the God in you makes you stand tall, bold, and assured.

Many may grind their teeth, and even taunt you because they witness the power given to you by God.

But remember this:

You walk with that bounce that only you can do.
Speak softly, wisely and with authority.

Expect greatness and miracles every day from God!

You were created to shine and nothing nor anyone can change your path set by God! Amen!

Matthew 5:16
"Let your light shine before men in such a way that they may see your good works and glorify your Father who is in heaven."

ACKNOWLEDGEMENTS

Howard Carroll, I thank you for being a supportive husband in my life. When I begin to doubt, you tell me why I can. You remind me daily of the power that God has given me to encourage others. Our love for one another is anchored in God. You are truly a blessing from God, and I appreciate you and love you.

A heartfelt love is extended to my parents, Garland and Shirley Dixon and Dorothy Ann Carroll; my sisters Sheretta Williams, Betina Brown, Anne Marie Sanders and Robyn Champ; my brother Roger Tatum, my cousin Michelle Leach (Cookie), all of whom at various times in my life have provided tremendous support and encouragement by their words of compassion and motivation.

Special love is expressed to my nieces Shemika Williams and Jerisa Harris and my nephew Kevin Williams. I love you all more than you know. You all are a sweet blessing to my soul.

I am grateful to Bishop and First Lady Roland Kenner Jr. and Terry Kenner and all my church family at International Church of Christ who have offered so many words of encouragement, prayers and support. A very special expression of gratitude for Mother Taylor who prayed and encouraged me during one of my darkest hours. I am not in this life alone; and it is a blessing to have so many hold my hand, laugh, and cry with me on my journey.

Romans 12:10
"Love one another with brotherly affection. Outdo one another in showing honor."

FOREWORD

Kimberly Dixon Carroll was inspired to write this book with the prompting of the Holy Spirit. During Kimberly's life experiences, it was words of encouragement that helped her to overcome challenges and reach higher levels in her life with God. The truth is that we all battle our own personal moments of self-doubt, insecurity, and discouragement; even moments where we feel like giving up rather than going on. Kimberly's writings are gifts of wisdom and encouragement wrapped in words of inspiration to motivate and enlighten her readers.

Kimberly searched for years for her purpose. Finally, God opened up the veil that was keeping her from seeing her divine mission in life. Kimberly's divine purpose is to breathe life into God's Creations with written words of wisdom and encouragement. Kimberly is grateful to God Almighty who poured into her the gift to draw people into their personal relationship with God.

Good Blessed Morning!

I AM HUMAN

Sometimes I am strong and sometimes I am weak. But all the time I am human. The greatest blessing to know is that we were created by God in His image. No man can take the credit for the power God has alone for speaking the world and life into existence.

Genesis 1:27
"So, God created man in his own image, in the image of God he created him; male and female he created them."

Good Blessed Morning!

A PRAYER TODAY

Lord we come to You, many with heavy hearts; while others celebrate moments of goodness and delight.
You know our needs.
We pray for open doors.
We pray for healing.
We pray for justice.
We pray for peace.
We pray for wisdom.
We know that You are the God of all creation.
We invite You into our hearts.
We want You to dwell in our spirits.
Thank You, Creator for the sunset to rest.
Thank You, Creator for the sunrise to be productive.
Watch over all of us throughout the day.
Hold on to our hands and don't let go! Amen!

Prayer is good, and it is our direct line to communicating with God. It is dialogue between our spirits and the Spirit of God. Through prayer we acknowledge God with our confidence and belief that our prayers will be answered. There is no wrong way to pray, just be real and come before God humbly. Sometimes our prayers can be silent as we allow our heart to open to God.

Psalm 17:6
"I call on you, my God, for you will answer me; turn your ear to me and hear my prayer."

Good Blessed Morning!

MY BEAUTIFUL HUSBAND

May the sun guide your every step today.
May your heart be filled with joy.
May others be lifted today because of your joy.
You are my delight every day!
I pray an awesome productive day for you!
Our husbands are so very special.
African-American men need the powerful prayers of their Queens.
The world was designed since slavery to separate the Black man from his family.
We need divine intervention to keep our Kings protected.

Ephesians 5:25
"Husbands love your wives, just as Christ loved the church and gave himself up for her."

Good Blessed Morning!

SWEET ROLL

It is not my hair that determines my worth that would cause one to stare with great care.
It is not my breasts that make me beautiful to welcome my guests.
It is not my posterior that projects my minds interior.
It is my soul and character that makes me a delectable sweet roll;
That caused my husband to fuse us, mending our hearts and souls together as one.

Psalm 139:13-16
"For you formed my inward parts; you knitted me together in my mother's womb. I praise you, for I am fearfully and wonderfully made. Wonderful are your works; my soul knows it very well. My frame was not hidden from you, when I was being made in secret, intricately woven in the depths of the earth. Your eyes saw my unformed substance; in your book were written, every one of them, the days that were formed for me, when as yet there was none of them."

Good Blessed Morning!

SOULMATE

There is no such thing as a perfect relationship; not by a long shot.
Your soulmate helps to weather the storms that surely will rage.
You will argue, disagree, and even shout.
And if we can be real for a minute, some shoes and clothes, and name calling other than our first names, may fly across the room.
But after it becomes calm,
heartbeats slow down,
emotions return to normal,
and the sweat cools you both down.
You both realize that life is with each other and no one else.
That is when compromise, listening, forgiveness, and understanding enter the relationship.
The right relationship never feels like a bad thing that has to end.
Instead it feels like a good thing that has to be nurtured.
This is what it is like being united with your soul mate.
You have your ups and downs.
And you grow with each other through each experience.

Genesis 2:22-24
"Then the LORD God made a woman from the rib he had taken out of the man, and he brought her to the man.
The man said, "This is now bone of my bones and flesh of my flesh; she shall be called 'woman,' for she was taken out of man."
That is why a man leaves his father and mother and is united to his wife, and they become one flesh."

Good Blessed Morning!

FORGIVENESS

You want to hold onto grudges?
Think for a moment about who you have hurt and needed to be forgiven.
Forgiveness is a beautiful spirit that embraces our universe and finds refuge in many different hearts.
We connect to one another's heart through forgiveness.
No one man or one woman walking through life, can take the credit of walking in perfection nor exclude the need to forgive.

Colossians 3:13
"Bear with each other and forgive one another if any of you has a grievance against someone. Forgive as the Lord forgave you."

Good Blessed Morning!

PACKED SCHEDULES

So many times, we want to make our schedules packed with special activities, people to see, and things to do. We post pictures of joy. Yet for many, behind those smiles are faces of hardship and pain. God sees behind our smiles. Amen.

Some fill unhappiness with so much "activity", we cannot hear when God is speaking to us. Sometimes activity helps us avoid looking at the pain, helps us avoid dealing with situations we don't want to tackle; helps us avoid making decisions we know need to be made. Some are lonely after losing their spouse of twenty-five years. Some need to put their foot down and say, "enough is enough." Let us face the truth, sometimes we hide behind "busyness".

I hear God saying to slow down just a bit and spend more quality time speaking, talking and in relationship with Him. When it comes to God, remember we do not have to avoid those things that bring us pain or fear. We can release them to God to receive wisdom and direction. Amen!

Psalm 46:10
"Be still and know that I am God. I will be exalted among the nations, I will be exalted in the earth!"

Good Blessed Morning!

GOD'S CLASSROOM

It is a sweet moment when God places you in a position where it is just you and Him. You cannot turn to Momma for help, sister cannot help, friends have gone, and hubby cannot help. It is you and God, spirit to Spirit. It is a moment of honest, raw teaching directly from God where we meet face to face with faith and hope. It is God mentoring, teaching, and coaching us one on one. We are the student and God is the Teacher.

In our classroom, God takes away all of our crutches that stand in the way of our complete confidence and expectation in God's Word. The crutch could be a job, money, power, position and or things. Our crutches misdirect our understanding of where all good things originate. Our jobs become our source of income. Our positions become our fountain of authority. Our wealth becomes our spring of power. These crutches blind us to the truth that God is the origin of all our blessings.

It is not of our own doing that we accomplish and achieve, but often we believe in the "me" syndrome, which is another crutch. We believe it is because of "me" that I have accomplished my endeavors. Yet the truth is that any source of income, any position of authority, and our ability to eat that which only the rich can afford are all sources of treasures that come from God.

It is because of God that we experience great blessings. We must understand that God is the origin of all of our prominent sources. Amen!

Be proud when God removes us from the general population and places us in our special room for one on one cultivation and teaching. Amen! Our trials are our teaching moments designed by God to be one on one with Him. Amen!

2 Corinthians 3:5
"Not that we are sufficient by ourselves to think anything as from ourselves; but our sufficiency is from God"

Good Blessed Morning!

DECEIT

Somehow folks get deceit confused with being wise. Some think that they have mastered deception because they believe they are wiser than the next.

It is the mighty omnipresent living God who sees and knows all and who is the wisest. So, when you lie or deceive who are you really fooling? You are fooling no one except yourself.

The enemy is laughing at your own foolishness because you are allowing him to control and manipulate your life away from God. His purpose in life is to keep you separated from your Divine Tree. Don't ever mistake that the silence of your victim or victims is your victory of deceit.

And do not ever think you have mastered deception. It is nothing glorifying about deception. It does not make you wise or smart. It only makes you a fool. The prime work of the enemy is to destroy character, and at any cost keep you separated from God. So, while you think you have won at being cunning, you really have only taken steps that are separating you more and more from God. God sees all and knows all.

And He surely is not going to allow His people, to be deceived, nor to be taken advantaged of without equipping them with the wisdom they need to come out of fruitless barren dry land and move into nurturing, luscious, fruitful abundance.

Proverbs 11:3
"The integrity of the upright guides them, but the crookedness of the treacherous destroys them."

Good Blessed Morning!

JOY

You feel like giving up because you gave your best and it is not valued by those who you love the most. But giving up is what the adversary wants you to do.

Negative energy keeps you from seeing the fountain of joy. The joy that God places in your heart; your joy is not dependent on circumstances. Hallelujah! Your joy is a gift from God that allows you to smile even during your toughest time.

Romans 15:13
"May the God of hope fill you with all joy and peace as you trust in him, so that you may overflow with hope by the power of the Holy Spirit."

Good Blessed Morning!

FILLED WITH HOPE

Feeling afraid? Remember Christ conquered fear on the Cross!

Feeling anxious? Remember Christ conquered anxiety on the Cross!

Feeling worthless? Remember God established value for all on the Cross!

There is no negative feeling or experience that God did not conquer on the Cross!

We are filled with hope, possibility, happiness, abundance and God's mighty Spirit!

You will succeed with each step you take!

John 3:16-17
"For God so loved the world that he gave his only Son, that whoever believes in him should not perish but have eternal life. For God did not send his Son into the world to condemn the world, but in order that the world might be saved through Him."

Good Blessed Morning!

SELF LOVE

Yes! We are to awake feeling good about ourselves.
When we feel good, we are able to love others.
I see myself as a unique creation destined for purpose and excellence! And so, should you! It is not arrogance but self-love.

Song of Solomon 4:7
"You are altogether beautiful, my love; there is no flaw in you."

Good Blessed Morning!

THE TABLE

Talking about racism does not spark violence or hatred.

Talking about racism and admitting to how inhumane it has been in the history of the United States is the beginning of healing for this Nation; not just for the oppressed but also for the oppressors.

Yes! The oppressors need healing too!

But because our society would rather suppress the truth, racism still lives and breathes in the hearts and minds of many.

Racism is a living vicious state of mind that is entrenched in the thought processes and decisions of very powerful political people in our democracy.

However, the table of learning, understanding, conscientiousness and forgiveness has been set for the oppressors; prepared and ready for the guest to come and partake in a meal of transformation. Our guests have yet to accept the invitation and take a seat.

Galatians 3:28
"There is neither Jew nor Gentile, neither slave nor free, nor is there male and female, for you are all one in Christ Jesus"

Good Blessed Morning!

EBBS AND FLOWS

You can make all the "right" choices in life but still experience opposition. Challenges can leave us feeling hurt, sad, and even confused; but they can also leave us feeling energized, confident, hopeful and confident.

We experience both light and darkness in our walk of life. The creator of everything tells us that in life there is a season and a time for every activity under heaven.

Our ebbs and flows are our seasons. Even when we don't understand the ebbs, God is with us to bring us through.

Live today knowing that God has you and will be with you in your seasons of flow. Sending you much love! Life is a series of epic moments of learning. Amen!

Ecclesiastes 3:1-8
"There is a time for everything, and a season for every activity under the heavens: a time to be born and a time to die, a time to plant and a time to uproot, a time to kill and a time to heal, a time to tear down and a time to build, a time to weep and a time to laugh, a time to mourn and a time to dance, a time to scatter stones and a time to gather them, a time to embrace and a time to refrain from embracing, a time to search and a time to give up, a time to keep and a time to throw away, a time to tear and a time to mend, a time to be silent and a time to speak. a time to love and a time to hate, a time for war and a time for peace."

Good Blessed Morning!

EYES OF GOD

What is it like looking in the Eyes of God?
It is experiencing Hope!
When your table is empty, and dawn is just a few hours away, but you rest well knowing that somehow your family will eat. In the morning there is a knock on the door from a neighbor giving you bags of groceries.

It is looking at your college invoice that is due today, but you don't have the money and you are in your last year. But you take your finals without worry because you know somehow that bill will get paid and it does.

It is looking for a job with no responses and a door opens for a job you did not even apply for.

It is the doctor saying you have three months to live and you have lived six years beyond the three months. Great Glory!

I think we all have looked in the Eyes of God several times
and experienced hope beyond what words can describe.

Psalms 32:8
"I will instruct and teach you about how you should live. I will advise you as I look you in the eye."

Good Blessed Morning!

GREATNESS

Being great is not the ability to trample over the success of others as our politicians teach us;
But rather it is the ability to enhance the success of the greater good.
It is our human connections with each other that makes us whole.
Your hunger matters.
Your tears matter.
Your laughter matters.
You matter.

1 John 4:7-8
"Beloved, let us love one another, for love is from God, and whoever loves has been born of God and knows God. Anyone who does not love does not know God, because God is love."

Good Blessed Morning!

JUXTAPOSITION

JUXTAPOSITION

The juxtaposition of a barren tree and thick luscious green grass should remind us that no matter the season we are experiencing, God always gives us what we need to continue to thrive, prosper, grow and experience life sustaining richness!

Philippians 4:19
"And my God will supply every need of yours according to his riches in glory in Christ Jesus."

Good Blessed Morning!

HOMELESSNESS

The United States should be ashamed of the number of homeless people we have while at the same time cities are experiencing revitalization and million-dollar one-bedroom condos are being built and sold like hotcakes.

There is something seriously wrong with one of the richest countries in the world allowing their own to go homeless and in need of food.

Isaiah 58:7
"Is it not to share your bread with the hungry and bring the homeless poor into your house; when you see the naked, to cover him, and not to hide yourself from your own flesh?"

Good Blessed Morning!

BARREN SOIL

When you live your life lying to your partner about any and everything consistently, and partaking daily in unproductive circles, you are developing a recipe of complete failure for not only your life but also your relationship. Understand that the one who knows and understands the value they bring to the table will not continue to focus or nurture grounds that have proven over time to be only barren soil.

Everyone wants fertile soil and I am not talking about money or material possessions.

Is it not common sense to want and nurture fertile soil that will bring forth an abundance of quality for life?

Don't think for a moment that the farmer will not leave and turn his back on the barren land after several attempts to nurture the land that has proven to be uncultivable.

Sometimes when we think we are out smarting someone we are actually making room for them to walk away happily and embrace the horizon in front of them. Life offers us many rainbows.

Galatians 5:22-23
"22 But the fruit of the Spirit is love, joy, peace, forbearance, kindness, goodness, faithfulness, 23 gentleness and self-control. Against such things there is no law."

Good Blessed Morning!

TROUBLED WATERS

It seems like we are surrounded by chaos and mayhem. Racism is showing its ugly head in TV stars and in our 45th president. Homicide rates are increasing in the District.

Children continue to disappear off our streets.

Yes, family our waters are troubled.

But when we listen to God's words, they tell us trust in God and not to worry.

God will see us through!

God conquered death, so we can be victorious over all that is not good!

Isaiah 43:2
"When you pass through the waters, I will be with you; and when you pass through the rivers, they will not sweep over you. When you walk through the fire, you will not be burned; the flames will not set you ablaze."

Good Blessed Morning!

ROAD OF SUCCESS

We are molded in this society to think that income, houses, and material items are goals to strive for if you want to be seen as successful.

But there is another road of success that is also rewarding; it is our ability to impact the lives of others in a positive way. It can take the hunger of an individual away. It can provide clothing to someone in need. It can allow the electric bill to get turned back on. It can help someone to read. These riches that don't come with glitter or shine seem to do the greater good in society. Houses, cars, jewelry, and designer goods are only for the eyes of others to see and to appease many egos.

Psalm 37:4
"Take delight in the LORD, and he will give you the desires of your heart."

Good Blessed Morning!

BLACK FAMILY WEALTH

Riding home yesterday with my Mom and Aunt listening to smooth rhythm and blues, I reflected on the three generations of women sitting in that car.

The older generation taught me how to love myself and others, how to cook, how to survive, and how important it is to have God in my life.

The family gathering yesterday touched me in ways it did not when I was younger. The infants and children have blessed our family line with continuation.

My prayer is that we teach the new generations about establishing family wealth. We begin to pass down real-estate and start new black owned businesses for them to own and run.

Laws, racism, and lack of resources prevented this for many generations. But God said the last shall be first and first shall become the last. I am praying that our new generations will become the first for Black families making their way to becoming a self-sufficient race.

We must stop being consumers of MK, Gucci, LV, gold teeth, $200 tennis shoes, and a host of other things and brand names that DO NOT empower the Black Family; yet receives our money.

I dream of towns where we purchase gas, food, toiletries, and clothing from Black-Owned thriving businesses but most importantly, we begin using Black-Owned banks for our financial needs. It is time folks.

Proverbs 16:3
"Commit to the LORD whatever you do, and he will establish your plans."

Good Blessed Morning!

RECOGNIZE YOUR VALUE

You know there comes a time where you step out in boldness; and say no more to walking on destructive paths!
You recognize your value as a King or a Queen.
You look back on all your mistakes and realize how they have made you stronger and wiser.
You understand and accept you will not be liked by everyone;
You turn your back to negative energy.
And open the door to the dawning of a new day;
You let the Light infuse you.
And walk only on the paths that bring health and happiness to your heart and a smile to your face.
You raise your arms and face to God waiting to be kissed.
Good Blessed Morning Kings and Queens!
Welcome to walking in your own light! It is going to be a bright day!

1 John 3:1
"Behold what manner of love the Father has bestowed on us, that we should be called children of God!"

Good Blessed Morning!

LOVE SUPPORTS

Love supports your whole being physically and spiritually; hate or your enemy looks for ways to destroy you physically and spiritually. Sometimes fun is a facade of true hidden dangers.

We are lured into smoking cigarettes when we are teens because it is a symbol of independence and being cool.

We are manipulated into thinking that because of that one hot steamy night that he or she loves me for sure. But when the night is over, he or she avoids you like the plague.

We are tricked into thinking that crack cocaine and PCP are just part of partying and that tomorrow we will be restored to normal. Yet for many it is the beginning of addiction and the beginning of a mind that can no longer separate reality from illusion.

Somehow our worldly reality of fun causes us harm in the long run.

Colossians 2:8
"See to it that no one takes you captive by philosophy and empty deceit, according to human tradition, according to the elemental spirits of the world, and not according to Christ."

Good Blessed Morning!

THE LAST FIRST

I have always been peculiar.

I have believed the opposite of society ever since I was young girl. I believe the marginalized are just as important as the celebrated.

Do you realize that this society refuses to recognize those who live in poverty as honorable people; Yet they have learned to survive in challenging times which have made them strong, humble and creative individuals.

Yes, many are economically challenged and are kept on the outer ridges of society. Let me tell you this!

God said the last shall be first and the first shall be last!

When you walk with God, you love those that society says to hate.

You have conversations with those who society tells you not to talk to.

You see the human in those that society says are nobodies.

Matthew 20:16
"So, the last will be first, and the first will be last."

Good Blessed Morning!

ALIGNED WITH GOD'S PURPOSE

There are things we want God to make possible in our lives.
I am learning that some of my desires may not align with God's purpose in my life. So, I ask God for what is in my heart and end it with "let your will be done."

I know that God is with me and has plans for me to prosper and grow! Amen!

Proverbs 16:9
"The heart of man plans his way, but the LORD establishes his steps."

Good Blessed Morning!

COBWEBS

Cobwebs appear in the early morning with dew covered grass.

You would not otherwise see the webs without the morning dew.

Once the sun comes up and the grass dries the cobwebs go unnoticed.

This reminds me that God reveals to us what we need to see at the right moment. Be open to what God is revealing to you today.

Jeremiah 33:3
"Call to me and I will answer you and tell you great and unsearchable things you do not know."

Good Blessed Morning!

ROAD TRAVELED

What road will you travel today?

Each day brings us a choice to decide where we will travel today.

Will we travel the road of promise no matter how our situation appears? Or will we travel the road of complaining and blaming and pointing fingers.

Look at our history. We have never been a people of failure even in the worst of conditions. We knew our God. We had faith in our God and kept pushing forward. What road will you choose today? I am choosing the road to progress. Will you join me? Have a blessed day!

Psalms 16:11
"You make known to me the path of life; you will fill me with joy in your presence, with eternal pleasures at your right hand."

Good Blessed Morning!

MY FRIEND

Once we are friends.
My heart belongs to you.
I am not above you.
You are not above me.
We walk next to each other.
I see your flaws; you see my flaws.
I accept your flaws; you accept my flaws.
Just like we accept each other's greatness.
We have a foundation made of a "no judgement" zone.
It is our space to be who we are with each other.
We pray for each other to walk on solid grounds.
So, I do not worry.
I will tell you the truth in love.
You will tell me the truth in love.
Even when the truth hurts.
I am going to elevate you.
You will elevate me.
We will be our best!
And all the love I have for you,
I know is the love you have for me.
We are not perfect.
And our friendship began in imperfection.
Even when we do not talk.
I think about you always.
You are my friend for life.

Job 2:11

"When Job's three friends, Eliphaz the Temanite, Bildad the Shuhite and Zophar the Naamathite, heard about all the troubles that had come upon him, they set out from their homes and met together by agreement to go and sympathize with him and comfort Him."

Good Blessed Morning!

GROWING OLD

In this society we worry about growing older.

This is because society's focus is on youth.

In the workplace, focus is on youth for energy, new ideas and lower pay.

We grow to fear aging and manipulate our bodies to represent youth by augmentations.

Aging is a natural process of life and it is a beautiful phase of life.

Contrary to our societal beliefs aging stacks up treasures of wisdom and beauty.

God in second Corinthians shows us that aging is renewing.

Embrace aging.

You cannot stop this beautiful process.

2 Corinthians 4:16
"So, we do not lose heart. Though our outer self is wasting away, our inner self is being renewed day by day."

Good Blessed Morning!

GIFT OF LOVE

The love that God puts in your spirit will conquer any and all diversity that you face.
It is when we step out of that light, we experience unrest and confusion. God's love is like no other love.
When I think of Dr. King and all the civil right activists,
It was God's love that kept them peaceful;
They were able to love their enemies.
I know there is no adversity that I cannot conquer.
We all have been given a gift of love;
It is up to us individually to receive it.

1 John 4:11
"Dear friends, let us love one another, for love comes from God. Everyone who loves has been born of God and knows God."

Good Blessed Morning!

BEAUTIFUL QUEENS

Queens we are filled with authentic beauty.
We are filled with God's breath of life.
We are adorned with intellect, and entrepreneurial visions.
Hard times give us character.
We never surrendered to any predator.
Life wanted to break our spirits.
But it was the cohesiveness of sisterhood,
That helped us rise with laughter in our hearts.
When we were told we were not good enough,
We turned to our Right-Hand man named God,
We will reach every goal planned!
Giving thanks to our Right-Hand Man!
It is not in our DNA to be kept down.

Isaiah 41:13
"For I am the LORD your God who takes hold of your right hand and says to you, do not fear; I will help you."

Good Blessed Morning!

MIRACLES OF GOD

Each morning on my walk I think about the love and miracles of God.

I think about how earth was created for us to enjoy, from the stars, moon, sun, waters and the sky, what we experience as day and night.

I think about how intricately our home called earth is designed.

Man cannot take credit for creation!

Thank you, God, for loving us!

Even our physical system from the inception of the sperm and egg is sophisticated; from these two specimens' life is created!

God You are amazing!

Your intellect is extraordinary and is miraculous!

And indeed, the center of all You did and are doing is LOVE.

We are always in awe!

Jerimiah 32:27
"I am the LORD, the God of all mankind. Is anything too hard for me?"

Good Blessed Morning!

OUR WEDDING MOMENT

It is five am, the day of our wedding.

I hear the birds singing and the house is very quiet.

The old-fashioned school house clock is ticking loudly reminding me that time is approaching. The coolness of the ceiling fans is keeping my butterflies still.

The next time I touch Howard he will be my husband the leader in my life after God. The next time I look into his eyes I will be Mrs. Kimberly Carroll.

I can honestly say without hesitation Howard is my soulmate.
We purposely sought to connect from the heart.

The feeling of euphoria is coming from a place of certainty and trust. The focal point is not the decorations, food, or the wonderful welcome of celebration that will surely take place.

But instead the commitments to honor, love, and respect each other as one. Today we become one under the eyes of God, our friends and our family. I have the rib that was taken from Howard to create me.

Romans 8:35
"Who shall separate us from the love of Christ? Shall trouble or hardship or persecution or famine or nakedness or danger or sword?"

Good Blessed Morning!

LIGHT IS BRIGHT

I am just thinking about life.
We look back a year ago and so much has taken place both celebratory and challenging.

This says to me to live each day taking in as much of the good life as you can. Life continues in the rain and in the sun.

Wake up knowing that although you may be challenged,
It is also going to be a day where you can still see the sun shining
Right behind the lightening and the clouds!

John 8:12
"When Jesus spoke again to the people, he said, "I am the light of the world. Whoever follows me will never walk in darkness but will have the light of life."

Good Blessed Morning!

WELCOME TO THE NEW

When God is in your life,
You are growing spiritually.
God is knocking down old habits and ways of thinking.
Don't ever think you are a failure with your walk with God.
God never leaves us, even doing our moments of feeling disconnected from God. God is always with us!

Keep pushing. The enemy wants you to think that you are inadequate in everything that God has for you to do.

Wake up with God and allow God to stir the Holy Spirit in your life every day!

Isaiah 54:17
"But in that coming day no weapon turned against you will succeed. You will silence every voice raised up to accuse you. These benefits are enjoyed by the servants of the LORD; their vindication will come from me. I, the LORD, have spoken!"

Good Blessed Morning!

WE HOPE

It may feel like things are crumbling all around us.
The surge of police brutality on Black people,
The deaths from fake marijuana,
High unemployment rates.
Elderly being attacked and robbed.
Racism running ramped in the workforce and throughout our society. Yet we hold on to hope.
We hope for change,
We hope for better,
We hope for more,
We hope for healing.
We also hope for happiness despite our circumstances.
Look for that light that is shining through the darkness.
It is HOPE.

Isaiah 40:31
"But those who hope in the LORD will renew their strength. They will soar on wings like eagles; they will run and not grow weary, they will walk and not be faint."

Good Blessed Morning!

UNIQUE

The most important value you can have in life is to treat people who are different with respect and acceptance.

Allow others to breathe their own air.

Have their own ideas.

Live their own life.

Acceptance versus condemnation is needed.

We are created to be different individuals.

Not to live a life of similitude where we walk around wearing the same things, doing the same things, thinking the same way.

Afraid to live outside the "norm."

Live in your own skin.

Be proud of who you are!

Psalms 139:14
"I will praise You, for I am fearfully and wonderfully made; Marvelous are Your works, and that my soul knows very well."

Good Blessed Morning!

RACISM

We will spend millions to see a Royal Wedding which does not impact our society. But we turn a blind eye to the teenage killings and violence taking place in Wards 7 and 8 in the District of Columbia.

There is no money being poured into these wards to tackle teenage violence. Yet we somehow can provide financial support for heroin addicts in neighborhoods that are predominately white, while ignoring the social issues of predominately black neighborhoods.

It seems as if the issues in black neighborhoods are not important enough to support financially with services. Yet the issues that arise in white neighborhoods are relevant enough to pay attention too.

We spend money globally to tackle hunger, housing, and medical care but protest helping the poor in this country.

Racism is alive, real and just as ugly as it was 400 years ago.

1 John 2:11
"But anyone who hates a brother or sister is in the darkness and walks around in the darkness. They do not know where they are going, because the darkness has blinded them."

Good Blessed Morning!

YOU ARE VALUABLE

I do not care how many mistakes you have made in life, you are still just as valuable as the next person.

We all make mistakes.

What is necessary in life is to learn and grow from our mistakes. When we look at our heroic leaders, they did not accomplish success without making mistakes.

They allowed their mistakes to take them to the next level. Don't get stuck focusing on a mistake. Recognize the mistake, absorb as many lessons as you can, and keep moving towards accomplishments.

There will be folks that tell you, that you are not good enough or that you lack what it takes because of mistakes. In some cases, it may be true because everyone cannot be a doctor, a seamstress or work with the public. In other cases, it is not true. Your perseverance will create excellence.

Take inventory of your skills and know your capabilities. God plants in all of us our unique skills.

Philippians 3:13
"Brothers, I do not consider that I have made it my own. But one thing I do: forgetting what lies behind and straining forward to what lies ahead."

Good Blessed Morning!

BLUEPRINT OF PEACE

You have the freedom and power to relinquish the guilt of always thinking you need to do things the way others demand of you. The history of verbal abuse, physical abuse, feeling less than, feelings of being powerless have ended.

You decide what it is you want to do without owing anyone an explanation of your decisions to do better and become better. You are now free to design the blueprint of peace and happiness for your life. You, your thoughts, your ideas, your opinions matter.

You are someone important.

Transformation is taking place.

You'll emerge as a new adult, renewed and alive!

Begin to live with joy and great expectations!

Amen!

Romans 14:19
"Let us therefore make every effort to do what leads to peace and to mutual edification."

Good Blessed Morning!

CONFRONT

Alcohol and drugs do not solve any problem. It gives a false sense of euphoria which is temporarily lived.

In order to progress or extend yourself to be your best you, you have to confront the problem(s). Ignoring or pretending that there is no problem only allows the problem(s) to fester and grow. You will continue to walk in circles, experiencing the same complications, dilemma, and obstacles.

Know the difference between "situational" love and "true" love. Situational love is connected to a benefit. True love walks with you in authenticity with no connection to a benefit. God's Love is ever present unless you shut the door.

Proverbs 3:6
"In all your ways acknowledge him, and he will make straight your paths."

Good Blessed Morning!

OUR BLACK MOTHERS

She is dawned with golden brown, mocha, crème, vanilla or dark chocolate skin.

She stands on the strength of God and ancestors.
She holds down the family, producing high school graduates, college graduates, and professional workers.
Pouring love nonstop because her love never ends.
Her warm hands healed our sicknesses.

She had soft strong arms that held us and wiped away our tears.
Her soulful meals satisfied hunger. She knew how to draw neighborhood kids.

She conquered all the negative assumptions of black women and remained true to self and family.

Her crown holds private conversations of wisdom nuggets.
When she opens her door to you, you walk into her castle, her abundance of love, strength, and glory!

Proverbs 31:26-28
"She speaks with wisdom, and faithful instruction is on her tongue. She watches over the affairs of her household and does not eat the bread of idleness. Her children arise and call her blessed; her husband also, and he praises her."

Good Blessed Morning!

MOTHER QUEENS

Mothers love unconditionally.
Mothers can make you feel you were the richest kid when she struggled to make ends meet.
Mothers are the pillars of society.
Mothers can ease your heart all the while her heart carries pain.
Mothers let you know that you are a shining star while society tries to describe you as less than.
When you tell Mama you can't she will give you five reasons why you can.
A mother always has your back at age 5 and at age 55.
A mother will sit on the side lines warming you up with her cheers even though it is rainy and cold.
But it is Mama's prayers that you never hear asking God to watch over her babies both day and night, that provides that blanket of protection as you play, participate in school, move to college and stand on your own.
It was Mother that has been with you from day one!
Happy Mother's Day to all of God's Wonderful Queens!

Ephesians 6:1-3
"Children obey your parents in the Lord, for this is right.
"Honor your father and mother"—which is the first commandment with a promise— "so that it may go well with you and that you may enjoy long life on the earth."

Good Blessed Morning!

FAMILY

This morning we are grateful for health and the coming together of new family members.
Family is all we have.
Family allows you to be yourself and walk in your own comfort.
Sure, each family has its disagreements;
But each member knows they are part of a beautiful dynamic,
And believes that God is in charge.
And understands that God is as close as a prayer.

Proverbs 22:3
" Start children off on the way they should go, and even when they are old, they will not turn from it."

Good Blessed Morning!

PURPOSE ORDAINED BY GOD

Life is not about seeking recognized positions of importance or a salary to pound your chest. It is about fulfilling your purpose ordained by God which is serving others. The joy that you will experience when your focused on the graciousness of God and your purpose will work towards the Greatness of God!

A true doctor who knows God does not pound their chest and say, "I am distinguished and should be treated with regard". Instead he or she is focused on their gifts of healing. They are fulfilling their purpose ordained by God.

The MBA graduate who knows God never says, "I got mine, and it's other folks' fault that did not do the same." Instead they will use their gifts given by God to help others get their degree as well.

God gives all of us the talents needed to live out our unique purpose! God guides us in love, and we should not become vain and puffed up but instead act as servants who heal, encourage, teach, moderate disputes, keep communities safe, and push healthy behavior. Arrogance does not result in anything fruitful.

Use your unique talents given to you by God to do the greater good for humanity!

Ephesians 2:10
"For we are God's handiwork, created in Christ Jesus to do good works, which God prepared in advance for us to do."

Good Blessed Morning!

JOY LIVES IN THE HEART

It does not take grandiose actions to manifest delight.

Some of the simplest things in life can bring you joy, like a picnic, hearing the birds sing in the morning, walking holding hands, sitting on the porch waving at your neighbors, going camping, or just watching the stars.

Happiness is within reach. Grab it!

Psalms 47:1
"Clap your hands, all you nations; shout to God with cries of joy."

Good Blessed Morning!

GROWN

Blaming has never forged anyone ahead. It has caused conflict and takes the focus off finding a solution. It is now time to think about what you can do to make change in your life. Once you hit the "grown" milestone in life, you are responsible for your own outcomes.

Ephesians 4:15
"Instead, speaking the truth in love, we will grow to become in every respect the mature body of him who is the head, that is, Christ."

Good Blessed Morning!

ALL IS WELL

Just when you think you will get a moment to breathe, something happens; the car needs fixing, the electric bill is higher than normal, you need new medications, that darn speeding ticket came in the mail and you don't even remember speeding, and kids' activities cost more than you thought.

You are still struggling being a single parent.
Well think on this. Take a look around you.
Not bad is it? You did pretty darn good in spite of your multiple challenges.

God brought you through somehow, some way.
Yes, six months or even twelve months from now you will look back and yet again be another witness for the Great I Am!

We belong to The Most High!
Again, look around you. God brought you through and will do it again. Stay encouraged and uplifted! You're already a living witness to the truth! The sun rises to give birth to a new day with new beginnings.

Matthew 6:25-27
[25] "Therefore I tell you, do not worry about your life, what you will eat or drink; or about your body, what you will wear. Is not life more than food, and the body more than clothes? [26] Look at the birds of the air; they do not sow or reap or store away in barns, and yet your heavenly Father feeds them. Are you not much more valuable than they? [27] Can any one of you by worrying add a single hour to your life?"

Good Blessed Morning!

ONE RACE

We should be at peace with one another no matter our race, our genetics, or the color of our skin.

Man creates division within the human race when we seek dominance and create levels of superiority whether it is racial or economical.

If we replace the greed of power, superiority and dominance, with the generosity of love, honor and respect as God the Creator of All intended, we would not be afraid to help those who are hungry, help those who are homeless, and help those who need clothing.

We would be mindful that the weakness in one man is the weakness within all of us. The strength in one man is the strength within all of us.

There is one race - the human race.

Mark 12:31
"The second is this: 'Love your neighbor as yourself.' There is no commandment greater than these."

Good Blessed Morning!

LOVE TRANSCENDS

Who are you to say who can and cannot love?
Love transcends cultural ideology.
Love does not fit into a pre-woven box filled with archaic sexual roles.

Love originates and creates as it lives between the lovers.
Love speaks each morning to the unpredicted pair.
It says, "Good Morning and enjoy the day you will create!"

1 John 4:8
"Anyone who does not love does not know God, because God is love."

Good Blessed Morning!

OUR VETERANS

Many veterans are homeless and without proper mental and medical care. They served and were dedicated to protecting our country. When they returned home, they were forgotten.

I hope that we become steadfast at implementing policies that show our true support for our Veterans. They need housing, medical attention, benefits, and support all around. It is unacceptable for any Veteran or their family members to be in need of anything!

Thank you to the Veterans and their families who have sacrificed their lives for our freedoms!

John 15:13
"Greater love has no one than this, that he lay down his life for his friends."

Good Blessed Morning!

NO DOUBTING

When you have a thought of doing something good for the community, don't second guess it. The thought comes from God and the doors will open to see it through. When you have a thought to own your own business, do not fear, the doors will open to make it a reality.

Fear and doubt will keep you from trying. If you don't try you will never know how competent and wise you really are.

Matthew 21:21
"And Jesus answered them, "Truly, I say to you, if you have faith and do not doubt, you will not only do what has been done to the fig tree, but even if you say to this mountain, 'Be taken up and thrown into the sea,' it will happen."

Good Blessed Morning!

GOD'S HAPPINESS

Have you ever met a person who's happy only for a moment?
They are happy when they get promoted but their focus turns to someone that received a greater promotion.

They are happy when they purchase a home but then become unhappy when they discover someone else purchased a more lavish home.

They are happy to take a vacation but become down in their spirit because someone they knew went to Italy.

This type of "happiness" is temporary because it resides outside of the spirit.

True happiness dwells within our spirit.
When happiness flows from the inside,
it matters not what others are experiencing.
You are happy for them as well as yourself.
This world cannot bring you happiness.
Allow God to fill you with true joy!

Romans 15:13
"May the God of hope fill you with all joy and peace as you trust in him, so that you may overflow with hope by the power of the Holy Spirit."

Good Blessed Morning!

BALANCE OF LIFE

This morning listening to the birds and the clashes of the waves on the beach, reminded me of just how elegant and nurturing life can be while at the same time it reminded me of the turbulence that we often experience. Life is not always smiling and laughter.

The rich live among the poor. Murderers live among peace makers. The good hearts live among the evil hearts. The Yen and the Yang teach us that that both darkness and light exist to bring balance. Yet, perhaps instead of balance it is just the way of life. The peace makers nurture, feed and house the poor and find those in need.

2 Thessalonians 2:16-17
"May our Lord Jesus Christ himself and God our Father, who loved us and by his grace gave us eternal encouragement and good hope, encourage your hearts and strengthen you in every good deed and worship."

Good Blessed Morning!

DAWN OF HOPE

Sometimes I want to throw in the towel of hope.
So much hatred in the hearts of so many. But I can't.
I have hope that we will live on this earth respecting and loving each other no matter our race, culture or sex.
We will one day truly eliminate the divisions of race.
We will one day truly eliminate the divisions of our economic status.
We will one day recognize that we are all part of the human race.
We will one day recognize that we were all created by God.
We will feed one another, make sure that we all have adequate shelter, adequate education and equal opportunity.
And we will rejoice in doing so!
I will not give up hope, I can't.
I may get very tired and emotionally drained,
but with each dawn I will awake with new hope.
I know it may just occur tomorrow.

1 Peter 5:10
"And the God of all grace, who called you to his eternal glory in Christ, after you have suffered a little while, will himself restore you and make you strong, firm and steadfast."

Good Blessed Morning!

PEARLS OF BEAUTY

The Beauty of Black Queens is not in our physical attributes,
This is grace beyond words; It is our spiritual and mental assets.
This is why we stand even stronger.
We have survived the raping of slave owners.
We have survived the separation of family.
We held on until death remembering the love of our husbands,
Taken away under slavery.
We survived the whispers calling us "angry" black women.
We have much to be angry about.
But we stood in love.
We allowed the light of God in our hearts to shine.
We survived for centuries, what would have crumbled the average woman.
God created Black Queens full of strength.

1 Peter 5:10
"And the God of all grace, who called you to his eternal glory in Christ, after you have suffered a little while, will himself restore you and make you strong, firm and steadfast."

Good Blessed Morning!

EMPATHY

We can end racism and many of the other "isms" that plague the United States. We can end it with something as simple as empathy. Empathy requires you to understand not only the other perspective, but it allows you to see your privilege, your bias, and your bigotry.

1 Peter 3:8
"Finally, all of you, have unity of mind, sympathy, brotherly love, a tender heart, and a humble mind."

Good Blessed Morning!

LOVE IS EFFORTLESS

Experience has taught me that you should not have to fight to experience love and respect in a relationship; nor should you have to compromise anything less than love and respect.

Love comes naturally because it flows from the heart where the spirit lives. God has provided guidance on what we should experience when we tell others that we love them and when others tell us that they love us.

Don't waste your life trying to make someone love you or trying to make someone see that you are worthy to be loved.

A true King desires to keep you at the center of his life and happy. A true Queen wants to nurture and care for you and keep you happy. Love is a natural process created by God.

Galatians 5:22-23
"But the fruit of the Spirit is love, joy, peace, forbearance, kindness, goodness, faithfulness, gentleness and self-control. Against such things there is no law."

Good Blessed Morning!

RESPECT

If we want respect in the black community,
we have to show respect for each other.
We have to stop the Black on Black crime.
We say, "Black Lives Matter."
Then we must stop murdering and harming each other in random acts of violence.
As it stands now, we are our own worst enemy.

Proverbs 29:24-26
"You are your own worst enemy if you take part in a crime. You will not be able to tell the truth even when people threaten you."

Good Blessed Morning!

GOD SEES OUR BEST

God sees the best in you!
Don't worry what others say about you.
Don't worry what others think about you.
God sees the best in you!
There are those who outwardly appear to walk right.
But inwardly are challenged.
You can hide from people by presenting yourself fashionably right.
But you can't hide from God because God relates with you from the heart. Open your heart to God and lasting change will come.
You will experience levels of life you thought unattainable.
You will walk in VICTORY!

1 John 3:1
"See what great love the Father has lavished on us, that we should be called children of God! And that is what we are! The reason the world does not know us is that it did not know Him."

Good Blessed Morning!

UNSHAKABLE JOY

We are nothing without God!
Look at all the glory from this morning!
How many have unmeasurable joy even though you are faced with challenges?
How many wake-up praising God even though you know your day will be hectic!
God places in our hearts unshakable joy that cannot be broken.
Know that you don't walk alone.
God is always with you.
Just reach out for that wonderful hand of love! Amen!

1 Peter 2:8
"Though you have not seen him, you love him; and even though you do not see him now, you believe in him and are filled with an inexpressible and glorious joy."

Good Blessed Morning!

BLACK LIVES MATTER

Yes "ALL LIVES MATTER."

But "BLACK LIVES MATTER" is bringing awareness about the truth regarding the unnecessary brutality and murders at the hands of white police officers on black males, at historically alarming rates in comparison to other races including the white race.

Don't distort the truth about what is really going on!

All lives do matter. But all lives are not dying at alarming rates at the hands of police for no reason other than being born black.

Genesis 1:27
"So, God created mankind in his own image, in the image of God he created them; male and female he created them."

Good Blessed Morning!

STAY ENCOURAGED

Often, we stop ourselves because we define the impossible with our thoughts. "I will never be a college student"; "I will never make that much money"; "I am not smart enough for that position"; " I will never be a business owner." Well let me tell you something. If one person can do it so can you.

As black Americans, we are forced fed the negative images about ourselves so early on by a system of racism that we carry these jaundiced beliefs with us into our adulthood. Yet, we must continue to rise and know that we are just as bright; just as intelligent, just as brilliant, and just as capable of being creative and successful citizens as the next person.

Remember this. The United States that we live in was built on the skills, intellect, and hard work of our ancestors who were slaves; but in reality, our ancestors were more than slaves, they were business leaders, business workers and inventors, who were denied their proper accolades. We are creative and smart people. We always have been. We have always conquered the impossible! We were inventors; scientist, engineers, and business people way before we were allowed to enter any schools of education. We love you Kings and Queens! Stay encouraged! Yes, You Can, and Yes You Will!

John 3:16
"For God so loved the world, that he gave his only Son, that whoever believes in him should not perish but have eternal life."

Good Blessed Morning!

MAKE YOUR DREAMS A REALITY

We often think our dreams and our desires are unreachable.
Sometimes we think it is just a crazy idea.
Yet you must continue to make way for your dreams.
There is nothing to grand for God.
God placed those dreams that never seem to go away in our hearts.
Listen to the powerful words of Matthew.

Matthew 19:26
"But Jesus looked at them and said to them, 'With men this is impossible, but with God all things are possible." Don't lose hope! But you can't get there without stepping out on faith and taking the necessary steps needed."

Good Blessed Morning!

WHAT IS GOD LIKE

We are made in the image of God.
The kindness that we provide to strangers is God.
The love that we share with strangers is God.
The encouraging words we share is God.
The beautiful voices that sing praises is God.
The overwhelming spirit that stirs in us during worship is God.
The sick that are visited is God.
The prayer warriors who pray is God.
Light and dark does not dwell in the same vessel.
The light can and is always willing to enter our spirits.
We must invite the light to come in and make our vessels home.

1 John: 1:15
"This is the message we have heard from him and declare to you: God is light; in him there is no darkness at all."

Good Blessed Morning!

REST DURING TROUBLED WATERS

Many are going through some hard challenges.
We are destined to overcome our challenges.
We must give everything over to our Creator and ask for wisdom.
While the storms are raging, God has put rest in our hearts.

Isaiah 41:10
"Fear not, for I am with you; be not dismayed, for I am your God; I will strengthen you, I will help you, I will uphold you with my righteous right hand."

Good Blessed Morning!

WE ARE BLESSED

I am blessed, you are blessed, and we are all blessed.
Don't give up!

Your future is outlined, planned, etched, decided upon, and predetermined by God! Amen!

What a blessing to receive such powerful words this morning.
Raise your arms to the almighty and receive God's loving words.

Jerimiah 29:11
"For I know the plans I have for you, declares the Lord, plans to prosper you and not harm you, plans to give you hope and a future."

Good Blessed Morning!

REMEMBER GOD'S HAND

Remember when you had no money, but food was put on your table?
Remember when you did not have enough rent, but it was paid?
Remember when your lights had a scheduled cut off date, but they stayed on?
Remember when your position ended, but you were offered a new job on the same day?

Remember when your marriage ended, and you thought it was the end of the world, but God ministered to you through song and held you tight?
Remember when you were diagnosed and afraid, but God stepped in and healed you?
These are all moments when God's hand was there to help.
When you start to feel discouraged remember those miraculous moments.
God is with us!

John 15:7
"If you abide in me, and my words abide in you, ask whatever you wish, and it will be done for you."

Good Blessed Morning!

YOU BELONG TO GOD

You are never a failure.
You may not have been strong today.
Set your goal for tomorrow where you will be closer to freedom.
You wrestle with both mental and physical challenges.
But know there is no obstacle that you cannot overcome holding on to God's hand.
Your freedom is sooner rather than later.
You belong to God.
Each day you will become stronger.
You are not a failure.
You belong to God!

1 Corinthians 3:23
"And you belong to Christ; and Christ belongs to God."

Good Blessed Morning!

IT IS NEVER TOO LATE

You may think that it is too late for your greatest desires to come true. But as long as there is life abiding in you, it is never too late to experience greatness and success.

Proverbs 13:12
"When dreams come true there is life and joy."

Good Blessed Morning!

GOD IS HOPE

I am just overwhelmed with the realities of our world.
How can I have hope in such horrific times?
Racism still thriving,
Teachers molesting children that they are supposed to be teaching.
Family members addicted to drugs and causing love one's grief.
People taking advantage of others for money or material gain.
It just makes me question my own belief about hope.
But quickly, I was reminded that hope is not a magical wand that makes everything right instantly.
Hope is knowing that God will never leave us.
That God will give us the courage and the strength to endure.
God will give us the ability to be at peace,
And fill us with love while the storm is still raging.
Hope will allow us to make it through the storms.

Isaiah 4:6
"There will be a shelter to give shade from the heat by day, and refuge and protection from the storm and the rain."

Good Blessed Morning!

CELEBRATE OUR LOVE ONES

Life is a celebration of our love ones in our circle.
We celebrate their smiles, how they made us laugh, their accomplishments, and their struggles. We celebrate their memories when they leave us to begin their next life in glory forever more; we celebrate their transition!
We must rejoice and be happy for them because they have been called by their name holding on to God's hand.
Welcomed by many angels.
Life in all its forms are a celebration of now and eternity!

Ecclesiastes 7:2-3
"It is better to go to a funeral than a feast.
For death is the destiny of every person,
and the living should take this to heart.
Sorrow is better than laughter,
because sober reflection is good for the heart."

Good Blessed Morning!

ALLOW NAKEDNESS

Fall in love with the nakedness of a person. Have them take off their professional titles and strip off their monetary value. Let the awards achieved and their acclamations fall by the wayside for a moment. Let go of the power they possess in the community. Release all the conveniences that are attached to this person.

Now stand before this person and become familiar with their life experiences. Recognize their belief systems and values. Seek to understand their level of passion for humanity. Sympathize with their faults. This is allowing one to become naked and temporarily dismiss any associations with monetary value and convenient opportunities.

Now you open up to favorable circumstances to truly fall in love with someone. Money, power and conveniences are the icing on a cake.

But the cake itself needs to include the necessary ingredients to produce a good cake. -- Belief systems, Morales and Values.

1 John 2:15-17
"Do not love the world or the things in the world. If anyone loves the world, the love of the Father is not in him. For all that is in the world—the desires of the flesh and the desires of the eyes and pride in possessions—is not from the Father but is from the world. And the world is passing away along with its desires, but whoever does the will of God abides forever."

Good Blessed Morning!

THINK OUTSIDE THE BOX

Sometimes you have to think outside the box. In business college we were taught that your primary goal of success measurement is your profit margin. I disagree, while profits are important to the life of a business it is not the only aspect of business success.

You cannot forget the employees that make your business a success every day, nor can you forget your customer base. When Howard and I open up our Laundromat, (speaking into existence our dream) we will focus on the reinvestment into our employees, our business, and our customer base.

We will manage with the understanding that dedicated employees at all levels, state of the art working equipment, loyal customer base and a safe environment will lead us to success.

You have to be willing to question and challenge pre-existing paradigms that only see VPs and CEOs as the most valuable in a company. Every ranking in a hierarchy is important; not just upper management, but also those who are in direct communication with the customers who support your business are also valued and should be paid as such.

Do not be afraid to step outside the box of what is considered normal. Don't always walk in a path that has already been paved. Take that shovel and start a new path!

Ephesians 4:29

"Let no corrupting talk come out of your mouths, but only such as is good for building up, as fits the occasion, that it may give grace to those who hear."

Good Blessed Morning!

PRIORITY IS KEY

Many in our community say, "I don't have the money for my child to go to college." But a closer look at reality, you see the very same parent spending almost $7.00 a day on cigarettes which is about $50,000 over a period of 18 years. You see parents indulging in the use of crack and powder cocaine daily, some spending $200.00 or more a day.

An even closer look into some communities, you see some parents purchasing expensive designer shoes and clothes for their child to wear to school every day. You see the same parent driving a Mercedes or BMW while adorned in expensive jewelry. Not to forget, women will spend $150.00 to $300.00 a month to keep their weaves maintained.

So, you see there is money for children to go to college it is just that there are other decisions being made that interfere in saving the money for your child's future. #blacklivesmatter and it starts with the parents.

Philippians 4:6-8

"Be anxious for nothing, but in everything by prayer and supplication with thanksgiving let your requests be made known to God. And the peace of God, which surpasses all comprehension, will guard your hearts and your minds in Christ Jesus. Finally, brethren, whatever is true, whatever is honorable, whatever is right, whatever is pure, whatever is lovely, whatever is of good repute, if there is any excellence and if anything, worthy of praise, dwell on these things."

Good Blessed Morning!

A COWARD IS NOT HONORABLE

There is an evil spirit permeating our communities. We see folks inflicting harm on one another; we are punching and spitting on our very own elderly without any remorse.

This negative energy could be put to good use by learning how to speak proper English, learning how to write basic business letters, learning how to write a business plan, gaining computer skills, or simply planning your personal goals. There are so many more favorable tasks to acquire that promote personal development rather than consuming our mental intellect and physical ability with wasteful, harmful and unproductive efforts.

Fighting one another and inflicting abuse on others are not acts of valor, but instead are acts of intimidation and that of a coward. There is no gain for our communities or for individuals when we act like savages without a conscious.

Proverbs 6:16-19
"There are six things that the LORD hates, seven that are an abomination to him: haughty eyes, a lying tongue, and hands that shed innocent blood, a heart that devises wicked plans, feet that make haste to run to evil, a false witness who breathes out lies, and one who sows discord among brothers."

Good Blessed Morning!

YOU WANT THE CIRCLE OF PROGRESS

When a person continues to stand in the same circle that has not provided any progress or growth, let him or her have that circle. You move on where God is taking you.

We are created for progress. It is so much easier to walk in circles without goals to complete than it is to plan, pray and walk towards progress. The latter is much more rewarding with productive outcomes.

Proverbs 16:9
*"In their heart's humans plan their course,
but the Lord establishes their steps."*

Good Blessed Morning!

THIS OLD HOUSE

I am sitting here in my parent's home reflecting in the room that I once occupied and "owned" as my possession. It's funny how when you have been on your own for quite some time, the home that you grew up in seems somewhat aloof. Not in a negative way; but in a progression of life type of way.

That place you once called home has become a place that houses many beautiful moments; some will make you smile and laugh while others help you see the progress made from childhood to adulthood. The old room says to me to visit as much as I want, but that should be the extent of your stay--visitation.

This old house welcomes you to cook, eat, even climb up in any bed to relax and nap, play, and even reflect. It lets you know that it will always be your home away from home. But at the end of your time, the aloofness lets you know, it is time to depart. Let Mommy and Daddy start their journey as empty nesters. It is now time for you to be the architect in building your very own home.

Proverbs 22:6
"Train up a child in the way he should go,
And when he is old, he will not depart from it."

Good Blessed Morning!

NO MORE EXCUSES

Excuses lead to no progress.
Excuses are no more than fabricated words joined together to sound good to receive get nods of agreement.
It is strategic actions that lead to success.
You must have a plan and take steps to complete the plan.
Excuses waste your time, waste your breath and waste your energy and you only end up stagnant and inactive.

John 5:3
"I can do nothing on my own. As I hear, I judge, and my judgment is just, because I seek not my own will but the will of him who sent me."

Good Blessed Morning!

WHAT IS YOUR CHOICE GROUP?

When you belong to any group, that group should enhance your appreciation for all people.

Their economic status or their professional position matters not.
If your group teaches you to treat others in unkind ways for any reason, one should re-think why they were so eager to join that group.

No matter how high you climb educationally or professionally, always remember that God is the Creator of all.

Colossians 1:16
"For by Him all things were created, both in the heavens and on earth, visible and invisible, whether thrones or dominions or rulers or authorities--all things have been created through Him and for Him."

Good Blessed Morning!

GREAT BLESSINGS

When your feet hit the floor,
This is a moment of a great blessing.
Be purposeful in what you do with the remaining hours.
Remember you are stuffed with greatness!
God is with us always, even when it seems like we are walking alone.

Joshua 1:9
"Have I not commanded you? Be strong and courageous. Do not be frightened, and do not be dismayed, for the Lord your God is with you wherever you go."

Good Blessed Morning!

SOMETIMES WE ARE PART OF THE PROBLEM

Take a good look at you.
How many people have you taken advantage of?
How many people have you hurt physically or mentally?
Who have you taken from because it benefited you?
Sometimes, we forget that we are often apart of the problem.
The next time you pray for others make sure you put yourself on the alter too.
It is easier to see the faults of others, even though we have a beam directly in our own eye.
I lay on the alter nightly. How about you?

Matthew 7:3
"Why do you look at the speck of sawdust in your brother's eye and pay no attention to the plank in your own eye?"

Good Blessed Morning!

THE MAZE

When all you can do is kneel, then kneel. When all you can do is cry then cry. You may be in the middle of a tenacious vortex-- that moment in life when it seems like every corner you turn is not the right corner. You are being tossed and turned every which way. You feel like you are in a maze and you're running and exhausted because you are trying to find the exit; but to no avail you just can't find your way out.

Hold on my brother, hold on my sister, just sit still and relax for a minute. God will guide you to see your way through. God is omnipotent! God is supreme! Our sun rises because of God. The air we breathe is because of God. The perfect balance of our solar systems is because of God. God is! Amen! When all you can do is kneel. Then kneel. When all you can do is cry, then cry. God is always with us! You will rise! The sun will shine! More importantly, the maze will disappear. You will have clarity! Amen!

Isaiah 54:10
"Though the mountains be shaken, and the hills be removed, yet my unfailing love for you will not be shaken nor my covenant of peace be removed," says the LORD, who has compassion on you."

Good Blessed Morning!

PEACE OF GOD

The Peace of God is a spiritual, powerful presence within your soul that calms and relaxes you while you stand in troubled waters. The Peace of God soothes you to let you know that everything will be okay. The Peace of God affirms that God will never leave nor forsake you. You can't buy the Peace of God! You can't work to earn the Peace of God! It is a gift that God freely gives. Amen!

You are looking at your immediate circumstances and saying, "How can I move forward? How can I smile again with something so permanent happening in my life right at this very minute?" Ask God for the Peace that only can come from God. Let God nurture your heartache and wipe away your tears. Let God speak faith into your soul. Let God wrap His arms around you and rock you to sleep. Amen!

John 14:27

"Peace I leave with you; my peace I give you. I do not give to you as the world gives. Do not let your hearts be troubled and do not be afraid."

Good Blessed Morning!

TRANISTION

People pass away every day.
Death is just keeping everything in perspective.
This life is temporary.
The good and the bad it is all temporary.
No matter your status;
No matter the position you hold:
No matter your riches everyone will eventually
Walk through the doors of transition.
The curtain to this life will close permanently.
Never to open again.
Do good while you are here.
Love each other while you are here.
Change what is wrong while you are here.
Impact someone's life in a positive way while you are here.

John 14:2-3
"My Father's house has many rooms; if that were not so, would I have told you that I am going there to prepare a place for you? And if I go and prepare a place for you, I will come back and take you to be with me that you also may be where I am."

Good Blessed Morning!

CRY OF THE POOR

Why do we spend billions for sports and scream about spending billions to assist the poor?
This is an outrage.
But even more than an outrage,
It is a cry heard from our poor all over our planet.
Please help us, invest in us, care for us, our souls are good.
It is just that we lack money.
Being poor is not a crime.
The impoverished should not suffer when the rich have so much.

Proverbs 31:8-9
"Speak up for those who cannot speak for themselves, for the rights of all who are destitute. Speak up and judge fairly; defend the rights of the poor and needy."

Good Blessed Morning!

THANK YOU DADDY

My Daddy was with me through thick and thin.
He believed in me. He demanded my best.
He taught me how to tell time, how to ride a bike, how to drive, how to count change which helped me get my first job at McDonalds.
The first tear I shed over my first love, Daddy was there.
When I was wrong, he told me and when I was right, he told me.
He took care of his family.
I had more than enough.
Thank you, Daddy, for everything!

Psalm 103:13
"As a father has compassion on his children, so the Lord has compassion on those who fear him."

Good Blessed Morning!

FEAR SHATTERED

We should begin to think of limitations as removable barriers. Once they are removed, we can see more clearly.
I feared not being smart enough to go to college.
Fear kept me from going to college for many of years.
But I put one foot in front of the other and sent myself to college while working fulltime and attending college at night.
I not only worked toward my bachelors I also completed my masters.

God gave me a talent to write and to use words to encourage and provide wisdom to others. I was afraid thinking that no one would want to read my writings. God removed my fear and I published two books. I removed that barrier of fear and so can you.

Psalm 34:4
"I sought the LORD, and he answered me; he delivered me from all my fears."

Good Blessed Morning!

EXPERIENCES BUILD

Yesterday coming home while riding on Metro, I saw a baby deer all by himself or herself. It looked scared and confused. As if it had lost its Mommy. Tears welled up in my eyes as I prayed for its health and safety.

Soon after, God placed a lesson in my heart to share. Sometimes we will experience situations where we are all alone. There is no one that can help us. Momma can't, daddy can't, siblings and cousins can't. However, just like that baby deer, these experiences will build us up!

Don't dwell on the negative that is within your eye sight; yet instead focus on the lessons that are present to take you to your next level! The scriptures tell us there is a time for everything. When these moments happen get excited about growing because it is your time for cultivation and improvement!

Psalms 27:1
"The LORD is my light and my salvation— whom shall I fear? The LORD is the stronghold of my life— of whom shall I be afraid?"

Good Blessed Morning!

THE OSCARS

There is an argument supporting the Oscars management team for passing over the actors of color. The argument says that it is discriminatory to nominate people of color simply because they are of color and do not possess the talent level of excellence in the elected categories.

This sounds like the argument for dismantling affirmative action. Affirmative action seeks to reverse discrimination against the historically disadvantaged in society which in the US has been the people of color and the poor.

What the management of the Oscars must understand is that the decision to avoid awarding a person of color an Oscar; has more to do with discrimination than any lack of talent. If you do not see people of color worthy enough to be recognized as best actors, best male and female actors, best film director and so on, many talented people of color are being grossly overlooked.

You mean to tell me popular films like Straight Out of Compton, Think Like A Man, The Perfect Guy, Selma, Wedding Ringer, and Supremacy, just to name a few did not qualify in any of the categories for an Oscar win? Some movies were even box office hits!

The lens of the judges needs to change. Yes, it is a shame to still have to look at possibly imposing affirmative action directives for Oscar winnings. Don't blame bad acting for historical repudiation of star excellence. The blame falls on the discriminatory lens of the judges. It is not only white male and female actors and directors that are worthy of an Oscar Win. Wake up Oscar management and become responsive!

1 John 2:11
"But anyone who hates a brother or sister is in the darkness and walks around in the darkness. They do not know where they are going, because the darkness has blinded them."

Good Blessed Morning!

FORGIVENESS

It is easy for others to tell you to forgive; they don't know what happened nor how the wrong doing has left you feeling. But forgiveness is not about the perpetrator but about you.

Anger that festers only keeps you from receiving your blessings. Anger could be blocking a new relationship. Anger could be keeping you from a new job opportunity. Anger could be keeping you from having new positive experiences and friendships. The one sure thing you know about anger is that it festers and keeps replaying the incident over and over again in your head. It keeps you stagnated unable to move forward. It does not have to be this way.

Exodus 14:14 teaches us that God will fight our battles; we just need to be still. As the well-known saying goes, "let go and let God." Inhale forgiveness. Exhale anger. One more time, inhale forgiveness. Exhale anger. As you move closer to forgiveness remember that you are not the same person you were 30 years ago. We learn and grow. Hallelujah! May the abundance of new experiences and opportunities greet you each day with each breath of forgiveness. AMEN!

Ephesians 4:31-32
"Get rid of all bitterness, rage and anger, brawling and slander, along with every form of malice. Be kind and compassionate to one another, forgiving each other, just as in Christ God forgave you."

Good Blessed Morning!

I WISH

I wish my skin was flawless.
I wish I had a big ole butt.
I wish I had fat legs and a tiny waist.
I wish my breast were smaller.
I wish I were short.
I wish my eye lashes were thicker.
I wish I did not have a gap in my teeth.
Then God said to me, "Oh My Gosh Enough Already!!!!"
God began teaching me that I am a perfect creation made by God.
Now, I love who I am and how I look.
Not only am I beautiful but I am unique.
There is no one made exactly like me.
I am a treasure shining on my own!
I no longer wish but cherish.

Psalm 139:14
"I praise you, for I am fearfully and wonderfully made. Wonderful are your works; my soul knows it very well."

Good Blessed Morning!

WALK OF SUCCESS

Images are powerful. I remember growing up and only seeing images of how complex and hard college would be as a student. I saw students sweating with stacks and stacks of books. I thought I did not have the intellect to pursue college.

I remember in middle school the administration wanted to put me in a clay and pottery making course and take me out of the mainstream curriculum. But my father refused to let this happen.

Well when I finally got up enough courage to attend college, I was 25 and working fulltime and going to college part-time at night. I remember very vividly my first night. I was afraid and nervous. But I told myself I could do it and I asked God to be with me. I first obtained my Bachelor of Business Administration and then pursued my MBA. It took ten years total. But I did it! I was on the honor roll in undergraduate and graduate school. It was not overwhelmingly hard at all. It took discipline, sacrifice and determination. And just think if I had gone right after high school it would have been a lot easier, especially financially because Mom and Dad would have paid for it Lol!!!!!

Images in the black community are communicated on billboard advertisements, Hollywood films, news media, and the like to purposely project negative images in the black community physics. To start, our men in particular are cast as people who should be feared and not trusted. Alcohol and tobacco usage to our young is projected as normal and acceptable habits to embrace and make a part of our daily community habits. Our women are betrayed as women who are angry all the time and over sexual.

You've got to believe in yourself, know yourself, and do not be afraid to walk on new paths and challenge current beliefs and traditions. I use my education experience not to boast or to be puffed up with pride, but to say to anyone that it's never too late to reach your goals. You can do it! If fear is present, walk through it and start. You can do whatever you set your heart to do. Take God's hand and begin your walk of success!

Isaiah 5:20
"Woe to those who call evil good and good evil, who put darkness for light and light for darkness, who put bitter for sweet and sweet for bitter!"

Good Blessed Morning!

OPPOSSING FORCES OF POSITIVE AND NEGATIVE

I think because mankind ate fruit from the forbidden tree of knowledge of good and evil, we will always experience opposing forces of positive and negative, of good and evil. But as always, God provides directions on how to walk with Him. We are given the choice or power to choose between entering the light or walking in darkness.

Look at the teaching in Matthew 7:13 - (Enter by the narrow gate. The gate that is wide and easy leads to destruction and those that enter are many.) The narrow gate is the part of life that is flourishing with affection, love and appreciation.

Yet it is the gate that fewer enter. Why do many more enter the wide gate which leads to destruction? It is because evil is often masked with smoking mirrors and the notion of amusement and power. In the wider gate, we are led to think that abusive consumption of alcohol gets you to that point of "feeling nice" when in reality, continued abuse leads to alcoholism. We are led to believe that crack cocaine will take you to this euphoric state of "elation" when in reality, its purpose is to lead to a chronic addiction. We are led to believe that sleeping with whomever and however many partners we please is being an "independent" man or woman, when in reality it leads to spiritual and physiological demise. Some are made to think that rape is empowering. We are made to think that spousal abuse is acceptable. The wide gate is not as it advertises. There is nothing amusing or empowering in the wide gate; through this gate we experience deception that leads to demise.

On the other hand, the narrow gate is not easy; it is hard work and there are no smoking mirrors of deceptions masked in the pretense of anything false. It comprises of the love for God, the love of oneself, others and the desire to walk in the truth and to want the best in life. The narrow door requires you to be driven with purpose to build up your neighbor, invest in others, and focus on community. It requires you to love those who look differently than you. It requires you to embrace the poor as well as the rich. It requires you to compromise. It requires you to fight for injustices. It requires you to look beyond self. So, while we will continue to experience the opposing forces of good and evil, we have a choice. We have the power given by God to walk through the narrow gate. God is with us and within us! We can choose Light! Are you ready? The narrow gate is open waiting for you to enter.

Matthew 7:13-14

"Enter through the narrow gate. For wide is the gate and broad is the road that leads to destruction, and many enter through it. But small is the gate and narrow the road that leads to life, and only a few find it."

Good Blessed Morning!

YOU ARE DEEPER THAN PHYSICAL ATTRACTION

When the only thing you have is your outward attractions to parade as virtue, you have already set yourself up for failure. To use only your physical status as supreme power diminishes and makes light of your own competence. Directly under your crown lies the pentacle of your own strength and wisdom which is the stature of the aptitude of your sovereignty. Our measure is greater than physical beauty. We are much deeper than a glance.

We live to be considered beautiful. Long straight hair. We even change our eyes to blue and green. We dye our hair blond! When will we realize that we are born beautiful with our natural kinky, straight and curly hair? We are born beautiful with our vanilla, toasted almond and coffee skin. Our lips are thin, plump and voluminous.

Some of our derrières are flat while others are what we call booty luscious. No matter the cubic measure or dimensions they help to put a little soul in our stride.

When will we realize that perfect art needs no tweaking, changing, adjustments or add-ons? We just need to walk into our own awaking of perfection. God made us perfect! Beautiful Queens that radiate love, prosperity and good will. Beautiful is what we are!

Psalm 139:14
"I praise you, for I am fearfully and wonderfully made. Wonderful are your works; my soul knows it very well."

Good Blessed Morning!

OUR FINE POINTS AND STRENGTHS

We are so conditioned to first see our flaws. But this morning, let us wake up seeing our fine points, our strengths. Walk in our own glory beaming with adoration. Are you someone that can lift people's spirits? Then celebrate it!

Are you someone that can overcome your challenges and see the good in each situation? Then celebrate it! Are you someone one that people reach out to for a shoulder to cry on? Then celebrate your greatness! Are you a teacher? Yes, celebrate your greatness! Are you good with budgeting your finances? Then it is time to celebrate you! Did you know that dreamers are the ones who visualize businesses into operations? Celebrate your greatness! Are you a great baker? Celebrate the sweetness you bring to life. Whatever your greatness, put it before you today, lift your arms and give honor and praise for your uniqueness! You are big, bold and beautiful!!!!! Embrace you!

1 Peter 3:3-4

"Your beauty should not come from outward adornment, such as elaborate hairstyles and the wearing of gold jewelry or fine clothes. Rather, it should be that of your inner self, the unfading beauty of a gentle and quiet spirit, which is of great worth in God's sight."

Good Blessed Morning!

GOOD CONQUERS EVIL

Sometimes it seems as if evil conquers good. We are reminded of the Civil Rights Movement; The Holocaust; The Columbine Shootings; The Virginia Tech Shootings. These tragedies leave us questioning our faith and even questioning if there is a God.

But I remind you that Dr. King did not look at the fire hoses; the Billy clubs; the spitting in marchers faces; nor the threats of death. Dr. King believed that God was a God of justice and would eradicate racial injustices. He focused on, God, hope, and faith. Hope is standing in a deep well knowing that God will rescue you even though there are no handles that will help you get out. You know that God will deliver you out.

Malachi 4:1
"For behold, the day is coming, burning like an oven, when all the arrogant and all evildoers will be stubble. The day that is coming shall set them ablaze, says the Lord of hosts, so that it will leave them neither root nor branch."

Good Blessed Morning!

GOD NEVER COUNTED ME OUT

It feels good that God never counted me out!
Society will throw people away like nothing; even after meeting several high accomplishments.
You may be feeling you're at your lowest.
You're tired, you know you can do better but you are in the ring battling with addiction.
Keep fighting your way to being clean!
God is going to use you to discount the judgements others have about you.
God is going to give you what you need to overcome!
It is you who pulls at the heart strings of God.
Society may have labeled you as a nobody.
Yet you are that diamond unearthed!
Silence the negative snarls of society.
Embrace Jesus who came to heal the sick!
There is no one walking on the face of the Earth who is righteous except God.
Receive the power of God and let God lead you to recovery day by day!
You are worthy, loved and valued.

Mark 2:17
"On hearing this, Jesus said to them, "It is not the healthy who need a doctor, but the sick. I have not come to call the righteous, but sinners."

Good Blessed Morning!

THAT GREAT DAY

After all the awards you achieved to be considered a powerful person,
After all the people you told that they were not good enough,
After all the evaluations you marked unsatisfactory simply because you had the power,
After all the tears you made because you had the power,
After you treated others with ill regard and only respected those whom you admired,
After you can no longer discredit someone because people have a way of learning on their own,
What will you say that great day?
When you stand alone, stripped of all your awards and anything important connected to this world,
And are required to account for your actions?
How will you argue for the tears you provided to so many others?

Galatians 6:7
"Do not be deceived: God is not mocked, for whatever one sows, that will he also reap."

Good Blessed Morning!

LOOK FOR GOD IN EVERY MOMENT

When I think of and experience spring, I always see purple flowers. Spring fills our spirits with excitement and joy because the harsh winter is over!

Sometimes we have to look a little harder for spring.
We have to see beyond the grey clouds and the tear drops from heaven to experience spring. If we look purposefully and intently, we can still hear the birds singing; we can still see the signs of spring from the buds on branches to the lush green leaves. We can even smell the freshness of spring.

We must see spring in our lives during our fruitless seasons.
We must know that God hears our cries, prayers, and examines our hearts even though we don't feel or see God working in our lives at the moment.

If we exercise our faith, we will see the outpouring of blessings beyond our current drought. We will smell and see spring.

Psalm 61
"Hear my cry, O God; listen to my prayer.
From the ends of the earth I call to you, I call as my heart grows faint; lead me to the rock that is higher than I.
For you have been my refuge, a strong tower against the foe.
I long to dwell in your tent forever and take refuge in the shelter of your wings."

Good Blessed Morning!

ANCHORED IN GOD

We are smiling, laughing and singing praises. All the while we are experiencing greater paychecks, being able to travel and see new places, our kids are behaving and doing great in school, new houses are being purchased, new cars are being obtained by God's children. But when we experience resistance and challenges, our songs of praise become silent.

Trials are just as much a part of our lives as blessings and goodness. When trials come, we can rest in the midst of our storms. We can be just like Jesus on the ship with his disciples when they experienced a violent storm.

Jesus slept during the storm. His disciples woke Him up because they were afraid. Jesus said to them "Oh ye of little faith".
What God was saying then and now is that if we are anchored in God we have nothing to fear.

Our song of praises should continue even when our own ship is being tossed in violent storms!

Romans 8:28
"And we know that all things work together for good to them that love God, to them who are the called according to his purpose."

Good Blessed Morning!

ENCOURAGE YOURSELF

Sometimes the hardest act to accomplish is encouraging yourself.

This, especially when you are at a point when the odds are against you at each turn you make. But find the strength and hope to be the greatest cheerleader you can to your spirit even when that job you have been praying for has not made an offer or your current work environment is toxic, and you see no room to grow.

It has been said that you experience great uncomfortableness right before your blessing. There is a career for everyone out here. Do not lose hope. Keep asking and believing that your door of opportunity will open!

Psalms 34:18
"The LORD is close to the brokenhearted and saves those who are crushed in spirit."

Good Blessed Morning!

NO LONGER A STRANGER

We acquire our tastes based on what we are accustomed to eating. When I started baking from scratch using fresh milk, eggs, butter, flour and sugar, we had to adjust our taste buds to homemade because we were accustomed to boxed and processed desserts.

So, while the homemade cakes were good, they just did not have the same taste or feel as boxed cakes. Are you all following me? Give God a shout!

This unfamiliarity is the same when God is transforming our lives and taking us out of the environments that are keeping us from growing and becoming the creation of effectiveness God intends for our lives.

Some of us build our lives in relationships with folks that do not help our progress, but instead help us to dig and pile up heaps of debris that causes us nothing but harm. Active alcoholics cannot help you become sober. Active drug users cannot help you become drug free. An active thief cannot show you how to have a heart for those who are vulnerable.

Like the correlation between a homemade cake and boxed cake, our taste and the acceptance for out new taste buds has to be acquired. We have to give ourselves the opportunity to taste better and to enjoy and accept better!

It is easy to pull out a boxed cake, just as it is easy go back to the environment that is so familiar. They are both quick and easy access. But once you allow time to show you the benefit of better and acquire the tastes of fresh wholesomeness you will not want to keep going back to old. Instead the better nutrition you receive in the new environment will have you walking on new paths of progress, positive intentions, honesty, breakthroughs and evolution!

Keep baking from scratch, your acquired taste will get accustomed to homemade! Keep walking in your new environment, time will allow you to feel right at home and no longer a stranger!

Ezekiel 36:26
"And I will give you a new heart, and a new spirit I will put within you. And I will remove the heart of stone from your flesh and give you a heart of flesh."

Good Blessed Morning!

WHAT ARE YOU THINKING ABOUT

Sometimes we can be our own worst critic. Somewhere along life's journey our eyes were trained to see the imperfect before we see the good. We want to start correcting before understanding what is right with us. Today I challenge you to see all of the wonderful delight that resides in you. I want you to celebrate your unique creation and what makes you stand out in the crowd.

We hide our differences, so we can blend and not stand out.
Not today, challenge yourself to stand out! Think on how wonderful you are and what it is that you are proud that God gave you and no one else. Today, as you move about in the crowds, let your unique light shine! Draw all eyes towards your positive energy.

When you look in the mirror celebrate the beauty you see!
Today is all about recognizing everything that is right about you!
You were created in excellence.

No "buts" today. No sir! You will see and celebrate all that is good and perfect with you!

Philippians 4:8
"Finally, brothers and sisters, whatever is true, whatever is noble, whatever is right, whatever is pure, whatever is lovely, whatever is admirable—if anything is excellent or praiseworthy—think about such things."

Good Blessed Morning!

MORAL CONSTITUTION

In the mornings we take time to shower, shave, apply our makeup and make sure our professional attire is neat, clean and fresh. We want to present ourselves to the world as credible, astute, smart, effective and efficient. Amen!

However, we should take the same care and nurture in dressing our inner spirits, character, values and morals. It is good to look fine, smell good and represent amazing on the outside. But it is even more beautiful to align our moral constitution with our outward refinement.

How we act when no one is looking should be the same charm, elegance and grace that shows on the outside. Our standards should be equally yoked physically and spiritually.

There is nothing more calamitous than a meticulous, well-kept outer person that houses a thoughtless uncaring inner person. It is equally important to take the time to nurture our spirits with God's Word every day. God's Word changes what others cannot see for the better. Amen!

1 Samuel 16:7
"But the LORD said to Samuel, "Do not look at his appearance or at the height of his stature, because I have rejected him; for God sees not as man sees, for man looks at the outward appearance, but the LORD looks at the heart."

Good Blessed Morning!

STORMS COME BEFORE THE BLESSINGS

I was reading the first chapter of the Book of Joshua where God was speaking to Joshua and telling him that he was getting ready to lead him and the Israelites into their promised land.

What stood out the most is that God told Joshua to be strong and courageous and do not fear seven times in this chapter. Sometimes we go through our battles and storms right before the flood of God's blessings come pouring down.

God will always fill our spirit with courage just as he did with Joshua. Just like Joshua we have to be courageous and not fear our battles. God will bring us to our promised land of rest and blessings. May you sleep tonight with an abundance of peace in your spirit! Your blessings are soon to come! Amen! God is always with us!

Joshua 1:9
"Have I not commanded you? Be strong and courageous. Do not be afraid; do not be discouraged, for the LORD your God will be with you wherever you go."

Good Blessed Morning!

TEACH ME

Don't teach me how to get high and drink alcohol like Kool Aid.
Teach me instead how to speak correct English and feel good about correct English.
Teach me that proper English is not a "white" thing but a "human" thing.
Don't teach me how to hang on street corners and around established businesses doing nothing.
Teach me how to be an entrepreneur, selling my talents and gifts.
Don't teach me that my priority with my paycheck is the liquor store first and drug man second or vice versa.
Teach me that home is my castle and my investment.
Don't teach me how to handle my problems with violence.
Teach me instead how to communicate and compromise.
Don't teach me how to beat my spouse.
Teach me instead how to love, respect and honor.
Don't teach me to steal like that is my value and worth.
Teach me instead how to earn an honest living working with my hands and exercising my brain.
Don't teach me how to depend on an economic system that wants me to live in poverty the rest of my life.
Teach me the various schools of intellect that open up doors of employment.
Don't teach me how to promote my body as if that is all I have.
Teach me to respect the creation God made.
Don't teach me to focus on my outer wear, or what brand name I wear.

Teach me to put priority on building my character, morals and values.

Don't teach me to sell poison to my brothers and sisters just to make my pockets fat with money and to think that I am living in the land of Milk and Honey.

Instead teach me the business acumen to run a successful entity.

Teach me what this society never wanted me to know.

That I am a great person and inside of me is housed excellence, intellect and spiritual power beyond any understanding!

Teach me about God who is Almighty and Powerful!

Teach me that I am created in the image of God!

Psalm 32:8

"I will instruct you and teach you in the way which you should go; I will counsel you with My eye upon you."

Good Blessed Morning!

THE FAVOR OF GOD

It does not matter that you don't have a degree. It does not matter that you did not finish high school. When you have the favor of God on your side, the things that our society count as material, important, essential and paramount becomes minuscule.

That is because God will place you on grounds that even you will say, "I am not qualified." But when God qualifies you, you excel, work in excellence, and forge ahead because God also gives you the intellect and wisdom needed for your new gift given by God. Amen!

We simply cannot count ourselves out when we compare ourselves to others. Throughout the bible God called ordinary people to do extraordinary works. The Disciples were fisherman who became fisherman of people.

The Samaritan woman at the well was an outcast and looked down upon by her own people because she was married multiple times and the man she was currently with was not her husband. But God developed a relationship with her at the "well" to tell her 'everyone who drinks this water will be thirsty again, but whoever drinks the water I give him will never thirst again". Many of the Samaritans from that town began to believe in God because of the woman's testimony about Jesus. Amen!

God uses those who are considered outcasts and ordinary people to do extraordinary things for the good of the Kingdom! If you think you are ordinary or outcasts, then I say, "Get ready for God to take you to higher heights that are unimaginable!" Hallelujah!

Romans 9:11-12
"God chooses people according to His own purposes; He calls people, but not according to their good or bad works."

Good Blessed Morning!

CHALLANGES

I think challenges are more about revelation than punishments. God knows the deepest intricacy of our hearts. God knows how dedicated and how much we love Him. Our trials and tests are revelations for us to see where we are in life; they help us to measure where we are in our faith. When our testing comes do we anchor ourselves more in God holding on to the promises of God or do we run, get angry, and complain.

Our relationship with God is about self-reflection and definitely about our growth in God. If we did not have trials how can we tell others, about our praise story? Do we truly believe that God will never leave us? Do we believe that God who takes care of the birds and the lilies in the fields will also take care of us? Will we cast our worries over to God because we know for sure that God is our protector? Our trial is a knock on the door, a revelation, if you will about where we are in our relationship with God.

Our faith in God should not stay the same as it was when we first accepted the invitation to Christ. It is necessary to grow in our relationship with God; any relationship needs growth as a necessity for life long endurance and fortitude. Trials are a true reflection of where we are in our faith and relationship with God. If we are not responding to our trials by being anchored in God, then it is an opportunity to grow and become stronger! Amen!

Isaiah 30:18

"Yet the LORD longs to be gracious to you; therefore, he will rise up to show you compassion. For the LORD is a God of justice. Blessed are all who wait for Him!"

Good Blessed Morning!

YOU ARE VALUABLE

When we open our eyes each day, we ought to know the measure of our value. None of us are without sin. Yet, Christ chose to die on the Cross so that we could have life more abundantly. This is the great value we have in God's eyes.

The person using crack and roaming the streets at night, God values you. The alcoholic still drinking every day, God loves you. The mother that has abandoned your child, God loves you. The person who lost their job and has given up hope, God loves you. The person who was taught that stealing is the way of life, God loves you. The spouse that is abusive, God loves you. Yet while we were sinners, Christ died for us. Amen!

We have power given to us by our Almighty God to become better. If we open our hearts and invite God into our lives, the oppression of the enemy has no power. We can walk daily in the power of God and see our true value. Drugs and alcohol mask our true value and often will not let us see the greatness of the person God created even while we were still in our mother's womb. We were predestined for our unique great purpose.

We were not created nor born to be a slave to drugs, thievery or alcohol abuse or any behavior that keeps us separated from God. As God's creations we are wonderfully and marvelously made! We have the power to live sober and clean. We are valued and loved by God.

Don't ever let anyone tell you it is too late for you to be who God created you to be. Each day that we breathe is an opportunity to position ourselves back with God. Every day is an opportunity to open our eyes to the greatness given to us by our Creator. Regardless of our sin, repentance reconnects us to our Divine roots in God. Our roots in God are where our power dwells to overcome any behavior that keeps us from walking in our unique greatness.

Open your heart and invite God into your life. It is time to reap the fruits of a flourishing tree and not the devastation of a withering, barren tree. Because God has power, we also have power. We were not created to be addicts, thieves, abusers or users. These roads are mere detours and distractions. You walked on the wrong road. We all have. But just ahead is your road God created for you. Get ready to exit and experience the love of God.

You have greatness in you. You are valued. You are beaming. You are amazing. You are celebrated. You were created for purpose and your steps in the Kingdom are ordered. Open your heart to God to experience your abundance and riches from God! God loved you and knew you even before you were born. Amen! Seek God and fulfill your true purpose. Amen!

Psalm 139:13
For you formed my inward parts; you knitted me together in my mother's womb. I praise you, for I am fearfully and wonderfully made."

About the Author

In life there are many roads to take. Kimberly is challenging her readers not to fear the road less traveled. It is on these roads where new inventions are created, new businesses are started, and education endeavors are achieved.

Kimberly took a less traveled road to obtain her Bachelor of Science of Business Administration and her Master of Business Administration. Kimberly attended college at night on a part-time bases, while working full time to reach her goals. She was older than the average college student when she started school and when she finally reached her ultimate education goal with the Masters in Business Administration. It was a 10-year journey for Kimberly to complete both her educational goals.

Kimberly believes that it is never too late to dream and achieve. The less traveled roads are the roads the majority of people do not take and are unfamiliar, but that is not an indication that people should not travel on them. Kimberly's writings are a way to motivate and inspire people of all races and genders.

Born in Evansville, Indiana Kimberly and her family relocated to Lanham Maryland at a very young age. Kimberly resides in Upper Marlboro, Maryland with her husband, Howard Carroll and their much loved two fur babies, Rocky (Puggle) and Sasha (Boston Terrier).

As you journey on the road less travel with Kimberly, her hope is that you find your connection to your Devine Creator. Kimberly desire is that you walk in victory and come to recognize all the beautiful gifts the Creator has poured into your being.

You are gifted.
    You are valued.
        You are amazing.
            You are beautiful.
                You are complete.

Philemon 6
"And I pray that the sharing of your faith may become effective for the full knowledge of every good thing that is in us for the sake of Christ."

Contact Information
Kdixoxnm@aol.com
301-257-6031

About the Publisher

At The Vision to Fruition Publishing House, we are dedicated to helping others bring their personal, business, ministry & nonprofit visions to fruition.

Whether it's as grand as a book you want to write, a business you want to start, a conference or event you want to host, a ministry you want to launch or an organization you want to start; or as small as needing a computer repair, logo design or web design; The Vision to Fruition Publishing House will help you walk through the process and set you up for success! At The Vision to Fruition Group we don't have clients, we have Visionaries. We provide solutions to equip others to pursue their visions & dreams with reckless abandon.

We have published more than twenty-three authors, several of which were #1 Amazon Bestsellers. We would love for you to join our family of Visionaries as well!

Learn more here: www.vision-fruition.com

www.ingramcontent.com/pod-product-compliance
Lightning Source LLC
Chambersburg PA
CBHW070919160426
43193CB00011B/1522